Foreword

    The Following Poems Were Written Between 1981 And 2000, My First 19 Years In The Circle Of The Nation Of Islam. They Are A Compilation Of My Thoughts And An Expression Of Emotions, Some Of Which Had To Be Overcome Or Mastered. If You Can Relate To These Thoughts And Emotions, Just Remember: I'm Only A Reflection Of You.

    I Can Thank No One But Allah (God) For Giving Me This Talent Of Writing; And For Allowing The Honorable Brother Minister Louis Farrakhan To Inspire An Entire Generation To Do For Self, Just As The Most Honorable Elijah Muhammad Encouraged And Set An Example For My Parents To Follow. For It Is His (God's) Words That Are Spoken Through Our Brother, And In Turn, Has Inspired Me To Write What You're About To Read.

    A Special Thanks Go To My Parents, Catherine And J.W., For Putting Up With Me, And Not Abusing Me, And Just Allowing Me To Be Myself, Regardless To Whatever I May Have Perceived That To Be. And of course, to my 5five children, James, Jihad, Marielle, Ansar, and Elijah ... now you know how your mother copes with life ... My Poetry is My Therapy ;)

    I Hope These Poems Will Further The Goal And Purpose Of Allah, Which Is To Perfect All Of Humanity And Establish A Kingdom Of Unlimited Progress.

This book *Black Consciousness Awakening – Poetry for the Revolution* contains Original Poems, Written By Sister Caryette Muhammad aka Yo' Sistah Muhammad

©1986, 2022
- YoSistah19@Gmail.com - (424) 278-4491 -
Includes poems from my first self-published booklet
"This Is It – A Book of Poetry" ©1982

All rights reserved. No part of this may be reproduced in any form or by any electronic or mechanical means, including information storage and retrieval systems, without permission in writing from the publisher, except by a reviewer who may quote brief passages in a review.

Published in the U. S.by Caryette Muhammad for Cary Designs, Indie Publisher, Los Angeles, California 90008.
ISBN: 9798847256773

Table of Contents

It's Now Or Never

From The East Unto The West

Thoughts About Saviours' Day, 1986

Songs To The Door Of Life

Words Of Encouragement

From Sister To Sister

We Must Revolve

No More Silence

Hindsight

Interracial Prejudice

Back To Black (My First Rap)

The Black Woman's Guide To Understanding Herself

The Time

Ah!! Peace At Last

A Glimpse of Heaven

Prayer

The Kingdom Of Heaven Is Within You

Soon

We Are One

One Verse, One Stanza, One Poem - Uni-Verse

All Women, Come Alive

Next Time, Produce A God

The Sun, The Son, The Light Of The World

I Am A Winner

Awaken The God

****

It's Now Or Never

All That I Have To Say

Is What You've Already Heard

My Poetry Is About Awareness And Unity

And Today,

Those Are The Magic Words

If We Don't Awaken And Unite,

God Will Wipe Us Off This Planet

If We Refuse To Build Our Unity On Love,

We Can Just Forget It,

We've Had It

Love Is Freedom, Justice And Equality

And You Know What That Means

Finding Out,

Then Performing Our Function On This Earth,

That's The Plan Of The Divine,

Supreme Being

All That I Have To Say

Is What You Already Know

We've Got To Unite Today

Or With The Wicked We'll Go
We Worshippin' All These Dead People
Who Were Indeed Great;
But We All Have Power Inside Of Us, Now,
So Let's Use It In Unity And Love,
Before It's Too Late.
****

From The East Unto The West

God Has Come

He Truly Has

To Bring Us That Which Will Forever Last

He Came In The Person

Of Master Fard Muhammad

And Raised One From Dust,

And Called Him The Messenger,

Elijah Muhammad

He Sowed In His Essence

Supreme Wisdom And Knowledge

The Teachings You Don't Get

From The White Man's College

Then The Messenger Raised His Disciples

Like Malcolm, And Farrakhan,

And Thousands Of Followers

And Took Us From The Mud Of This World

In Which We Were Wallowers

He Taught Us How To Eat To Live,

As Jesus Came To Give Us Life

He Taught Us How To Walk Through

The Valley Of The Shadow Of Death (America),

And Now We Don't Carry So Much As A Pin-Knife

Many Try To Destroy

The Wisdom Being Taught,

But You Can't Destroy A God-Send,

We Can't Be Bought

You Should Think Again

Who Concocted The Various Religions

Our People Are In?

Does It Make You Love Yourself And Your Kind?

Or Does It Teach You To Reach

For Something In The Sky

Something You Can't Prove,

And Actually, You'll Never Find?

When We Become Ten Thousand Actively Strong,

Then You'll See Why Right,

Is Never Wrong!!

****

Thoughts About Saviours' Day 1986

You Know,

I Can Understand

How My Brother Farrakhan Feels

To Go Away, Get More Wisdom,

Come Back,

And Everybody Else Still Ain't Got Real

It Makes You Feel Like

You're All Alone

On A Planet Full Of Life

But While You're Growing,

Everybody's Standing Still

Moping Over Their Misery And Strife

Brother Farrakhan,

I Left My City, Went To Hear Those

Good Words On Saviours' Day

And When I Returned,

I Felt I'd Grown In Knowledge,

Grown In Understanding,

But Everybody Else Seemed

The Same Old Way

I Said, "What's Happening?

Am I In The Twilight Zone?

I Know We All Got The Same Call,

But Only A Few Of Us

Answered The Phone?!"

He Ain't Asking Us To Do Nothing

That Is Too Hard

Say Our Prayers, Love Each Other,

And Put Those Of Us Together

That Have Come Apart

Allah Don't Owe Us Nothing,

Not Even The Air We Breath

So We Better Get Up

And Start Working Like The Ants,

The Birds, And The Bees

Now I Know We Ain't Got Much Money,

And We Are All Trying To Just Make

Each Day Through

Nevertheless, I'm Determined

That I'm Gonna Write Poetry

To Get The Word Out To The People,

So You'd Better Decide

What You're Gonna Do

He Put Us On This Planet

So We Can Enjoy Life

And Leave Our Signature On This Creation

So When Our Children Grow Up,

They Can Say,

"Look At What Allah

Allowed Our Parents To Leave Us

This Is Some Mighty Nation!!"

****

Songs To The Door Of Life

Where Are All The Singers

Who Used To Sing

Of What's Happening Today?

Have Their Hopes And Dreams

Been Deferred,

And Like A Flower, Withered Away?

Songs Like Yes, We Can, Can

Ball Of Confusion

And What's Goin' On

Say It Loud, I'm Black And I'm Proud

And Bring The Boys Home

Songs That Lifted The Spirit

And Made You Wanna Dance

To A Happy Beat

Songs Like Wake Up Everybody,

And Keep Your Head To The Sky

Were, Oh, So Sweet

If I Could, I Should, I Would

Throw Most Of These New Lyrics

In The Gutter

But Usually All The Oppressor

Will Distribute And Promote Is Trash,

And The Average Negro Don't Care

'Cause That's His Bread And Butter

The Rich Get Richer

Off Money, Money, Money,

And That's The Way Of The World

But I Remember Innervisions,

Smilin' Faces,

And Oh Yes, Be My Girl

Naw, I Ain't Forgot About

The Gospel Writers

They Doin' What They

Think They Should

But Everybody Don't Wanna

Listen To That All The Time,

'Cause Jesus Wasn't The Only Prophet

Who Did Good

So If You're Living For The City,

And You Trying To Get Solid As A Rock,

Don't Let This Cold World

Get You Down

You See,

This Is The Day We'll Have

A Harvest For The World,

Like A Family Reunion,

'Cause Ain't No Stoppin' Us Now!!

****

Universality

This Is Black

The Color Of A Nationality Of A People

What You See When Your Eyes Are Closed

The Core Of The Earth

An Ignorant Mind

Outer Space

Inside The Womb

Black Isn't National,

It's Universal.

****

Asia / Africa

Take Me Back

Take Me Back To Africa

The Motherland

Where All Life Started

Started With The Black Woman And Man

When I Was There, Everything Was Free

The Lions, The Birds,

The Gold, The Diamonds

Even The Bananas On The Tree

When I Was There,

My Brothers Watched Out For Me

Never To Worry About Thieves,

Never To Worry About Basic Needs

'Cause The Land Is Rich In The Motherland

I Want To Go Back

Back To Africa

Where All Is Peace

And All Is Free.

****

Words Of Encouragement

To Our Graduating Brothers And Sisters,

The Future Rulers

Of A New World Order

Now That You Have Completed

One Phase Of Your Development,

The Nation Of Islam Salutes You

And Encourages You To

Continue Your Self-Improvement

We Know That It Is Difficult

To Be A Muslim In The Schools

Of This System

The Peer Pressure,

The Drugs, The Immorality,

And The Absence Of Self-Knowledge

And God's Wisdom

But Hang In There,

And Be Determined That You Will

Turn This Wicked World Around

Become Dedicated To A Way Of Life

That Will Resurrect Your People,

People Who Have Been Lost,

But Are Now Found

Persevere To Become All You Can

To Build The Kingdom Of God

On This Earth

In Your Study Of

Math, Science, And Literature,

Use Your God Mind To Understand It,

And You Will See Its True Worth

Plus, Work On Making A Job

For Yourself

Don't Graduate And Give Your Learning

Back To Someone Other Than Your Kind And Self

Keep The Money In The Family

For Eternal Wealth

It's Only A Matter Of Establishing Trust

And Ridding Your Mind Of

Pettiness And Bad Thoughts

It's Already Written That You'll Succeed

And Correct The World's Faults

So As You Go On To Another Level Of
Understanding And Self-Development,
Open Your Mind To Truth
Study And Determine What It Takes
To Build A Righteous Government
Make Your Meeting With God
Your Main Objective And Goal
And You Will See That The Trials
You've Experienced As A Youth,
Is For The Good Of Humanity,
And The Perfection Of
Your Heart, Mind, Body, And Soul.

****

From Sister To Sister

Hey, My Sister,

We've Got A Lot To Do

Our Man Is Not In Power Right Now,

And The One Who Is,

Is Using Us To Keep Him Under A Shoe

It's Been Heard And It's Been Said

That The Black Woman Is Asleep,

But The Black Man Is Dead

Remember The Parable,

"Kill The Boys, And Spare The Girls"?

We're Living In Egypt Right Now,

My Sister,

We're Living In Pharaoh's World

Now You Know Where We Stand

A Nation Can Rise

No Higher Than Its Woman

So Let's Elevate Our Minds,

And Teach Our Children

The Glory Of God Without And Within

Let's Wake Up

From Our 50 Thousand Year Sleep

So We'll Produce Children

Who'll Build The Sphinx, The Pyramids,

And All The Great Ancient Wonders Again

I Know It Ain't As Easy As It Sounds

But That Trick Called

Divide And Conquer,

We've Got To Break That Wall Down

We Raise Our Children

To Call Themselves Different Things

You Say, "I'm A Christian, I'm A Muslim,

I'm A Baptist, I'm A Nationalist,

I'm A Witness, I'm A Rasta,

And I Can't Unite With You

'Cause You Don't Sing

The Same Song I Sing"

We May Have Come Here

On Different Ships,

But We Are All In The Same Boat

Now, That Has A Nice Ring

It Seems Like A Vicious Cycle,

A Problem That Can't Be Solved

But Love For Each Other

What You Love For Yourself,

And You'll See,

Our Unity Will Rotate And Evolve

We All Can Agree

That It's Time To Establish

God's Kingdom On Earth

So Let's Put Our Talents Together,

Manifest Our Ideas,

And Show This Devil That What He Built

Ain't Nothing But Dirt!!

My Sister,

There Is One More Thing

I've Got To Remind You Of

Since We Are, Now, Aware

Of The Condition Of Our Men,

Let's Boost Their Ego,

Dress Dignified,

Say Kind Words,

And You'll See That This New World

Will Be Built On Pure Love.

****

We Must Revolve

This Is A Poem About Revolution
The Revolution Won't Be Televised
Yeah, Niggas Is Scared Of Revolution
It's Hard To Win A Revolution
With Just A Gun,
'Cause Most Times The Enemy's
Got A Bigger One
You Can't Fight A Revolution
In Love With Yo' Foe,
'Cause He'll Offer You
False Friendship,
And That Revolutionary Mind Will Go,
You Guessed It, Out The Doe'
To Fight A Revolution,
You Need Some Type Of Discipline
'Cause When You Get Hungry,
Your Enemy Will Offer You
A Bowl Of Soup,
And You'll Tell Him,

"All Man, I Way Just Jivin'"

You Must First Fight A Revolution

With What The People Need And Use

They Need Strong Examples,

Money, Jobs And Dignified Schools

So First I Gotta Have A Good Home

Learn To Love The People

I'm Fighting For

Build A Strong Base

You Come To Me Talking About Revolution Before I Get The Necessities Of Life,

I'm Gonna Tell You To

Get The Hell Outta My Face!

Now You May Not Agree With All I Say,

But When The Fighting Break Out,

Can You Say, "I'm Ready Today??"

So Supply The People

With The Necessities Of Life,

And They Will Revolve

And Then The People

Will Revolt With You Overnight

'Cause All Their Needs Will Be Solved

Don't Tell Me You're A Revolutionary

And Can't Provide Me

With Clothing, Shelter And Food

'Cause The Enemy Will Come In With His Tanks,

And Nuclear Bombs,

And Just Go

Boom!!!!!!!!!!!

****

No More Silence

If We Could Tell Our Story

To The World,

We Could Make A Brass Monkey Cry

The Jews Bombard Yo' Mind

With Their Suffering

They Lost Six Million,

But We Lost 100 Million

In The Middle Passage Alone

Now For Whom Should You Cry,

Cry,

Cry For Us

Cry About The Slave Girl

Whose Child Was Sold

Before He Left The Womb

For The Slave Boy Who Was Lynched

And Castrated In Front Of Devils

Partying Around His Body,

Passing His Testicles

Oh Yeah, If We Could Tell Our Story

Tell About The Time

The Child Had To Watch His Momma

Nanny Masta's Child,

While His Three Day Old Sibling Wined,

And The House Negro Dined,

In The Back,

And Threw Out The Slop

To The Human Dogs

Oh Yeah, If We Could Tell Our Story

About The Pregnant Winch

Who Was Laid On Stage In Front Of All,

And The Devil Stomped Her Future

Into The Past, With His Football Spikes

'Cause She Said, "No"!!!

And What About

When They Hitched Another Woman

With Child

To Two Horses

One Leg Tied To Each Horse

Then

Smack!!!!

They Say She Split,

And Out Popped The Unborn,

Unborn!!!!!

And You Want Me To Cry About

Jew-Skin Hand Bags

They Don't Own

The Monopoly On Suffering

If We Could Tell Our Story On NBC,

ABC, CBS, PBS, CNN, NBN, WLBS, KACE

And More

And Now Some Folks Think They Free??!!??!!

Who Blinded Yo' Eyes??

That Damn TV

Fool!!!!

Gave Up The Revolution

Because The Devil Said To

You Ain't Forgot Who The Devil Is

Have You??

He Ain't Changed,

No Matter How Much You Love Them

And Marry Then

And Adopt Their Disgusting Ways

But They Only Getting You To Do

What You Really Wanna Do

'Cause You Don't Think

You Can Do Any Better

And You Think Their Ice Is Colder

And Now, Like Then,

You'll Fight Their Overt

And Covert And Subvert And CIA

And Contra And Gulf Wars

Just For The Money

And The So-Called Security

Oh Yeah, We've Got A Story To Tell

About The Black Soldier

And If We Could Tell Our Story

Of Today, In The 1990's,

Of The Brother Who Was Castrated

And Hanged To A Tree,

And They Said It Was Suicide, Up North,

In Klan Country

Now Whitey Says, "Am I To Blame

For What My Fathers Did?"

And I Say Will You Live And Die

To Change What Your Fathers Did?

Will You Let The World See How You

Hate, Hate, Hate,

To

Love, Love, Love

Blacks

All Over The Planet???

Naw!!!!

'Cause If You Love Us,

You See White Genetic Annihilation

Oh Yeah,

Yo' Forked Tongue's

About To Be Chopped Off

By The Bloods,

The Disciples,

The Warlords,

And The Crips

So You Better Try Hard To Keep Us Doped Up,

With No Hope Up In Our Heads,

Because When We Wake Up,

Your World's Just As Good As Dead,

And Then,

The Brass Monkey Will Smile!

****

Hindsight

I Remember The 60's

Coming Up In Detroit

How Could I Forget?

That Time When My Uncle Billy

Looted The Corner Store

And Got Home To Discover

That He'd Taken Some Baby Crackers

Instead Of Chocolate Chips

The Black Panthers On Mack Avenue

Between Lemay And Montclair

They Used To Call Me Sister

I Felt Good 'Cause

My Mother Had Me First

And It Felt Good

To Have Some Big Brothers

The Panthers Used To Drill,

Left,

Left,

Left Right Left

Ooom, Ooom Gahwah,

We Got That Soul Power!

Black Is Beautiful,

Brown Is Hip,

Yellow Is Mellow,

And White Ain't Shit!!

I Remember The 60's

The Brother With

The Muhammad Speaks To You,

And Bean Pies,

And Dashikis

My Daddy Had One Made

For The Whole Family

We Looked So Good, Psychedelic Down,

Afros High, Fly,

I Remember Those Days Gone By

And When They Landed On The Moon

My Grandma Said,

"They Ain't On No Moon"

I Remember The 60's

And What About The Tunes

The Music Of That Time

So Supreme,

Conjuring Up All Of Your Temptations

Producing Nothing But Miracles

And A Great Wonder

So Many Good Times,

So Much Sad Times

War!!!!

What Was It Good For????

I Remember That About The 60's

And So Much More

****

Interracial Prejudice

Hey???!!!

Before Spike Lee's Movie,

"School Daze",

I Never Knew How Much Division

There Is Amongst Us Because Of

Our Various Shades Of Blackness

It Never Before Dawned On Me

That The Majority Think

That If You Are Light And Bright,

That You Are More Alright

Than The Chocolate, And The Dark Brown,

And The Not Too Light

How Petty Can We Be??

One Ounce Of The Blood Makes You Whole;

From The Same Family

The Dominant Gene Should Rule,

Can't You See!!!????,

Or Are You Too Scared

To Challenge The Ones Who Programmed Us

To Quarrel Over The Color Of Our Skin,

Or The Texture Of Our Hair,

Or The Shape Of Our Nose

Hey!!!

I'm Just Proud To Be A Part Of

The Original Rainbow

****

Back To Black (My First Rap)

Back To Black,

That's What I Say

Back To Black, It's The Only Way

It's The Only Way That We Can Be

One People And One Humanity

You May Be Brown, Yellow,

White Or Red

But If You Go To Your Roots,

Then You Know What's Ahead

It's Back To Black, That What I Say

Back To Black, It's The Only Way

Back To Black, Back To Black,

Back To Black

There Ain't Nothing Bad About Black

'Cause Every Color Comes From That

And If You Doubt What I Say,

Then Keep On Living

And You'll See The Day

When We Get

Back To Black, Back To Black,

Back To Black

The Black Produced It All

From Triple Darkness To Albinism

But We Had A Little Fall

And Allowed The White

To Produce This Schism

But Now We've Got Enough Knowledge

To Erase The Philosophies

Of This Devil's College

From Yale To Princeton To Ucla,

Even Al-Ahzar And Timbuktu

Better Get Back To Black

It's The Only Way

To Benefit Me And To Benefit You

When We Keep Changing Our Names

Others Wonder

What Our Trip's All About

So You So-Called Leaders

Stop Confusing The Issue

And Playing Games

Because You Know

That Without A Doubt

We Gotta Get

Back To Black, Back To Black,

Back To Black

I'm Talking Strong

'Cause Truth Gives You Courage

I'm Not Just An African American,

So That Term I Will Discourage

You Can't Limit Us By Territory Or Turf

'Cause What Belongs To Us

Is The Entire Earth

And The Universe

So The Term Black

Gives Me A Better Connection

Now Take This Advice

And Take This Correction

And Get

Back To Black, Back To Black,

Back To Black

Negro, Colored, Afro American

The Bottom Line Is

That You're Either A White Man

Or A Black Man

The Reason I Make It So Simple And Plain

'Cause Everything Of Color

Came From The Same

We Finna Get Back To Black,

And That's Good

Don't Fight The Word,

You Know We Should

Get Back To Black, That's What I Say

Back To Black, It's The Only Way

The Only Way That I Can See

For Us To Rise And Be Truly Free

Black Is Not Just A Skin Color

But It Is The Real Mother

Of A State Of Mind That Says

That All Of Hue-Manity

Is Your Blood Brother

So Brothers And Sisters,

I Know What This World Is Coming To

It's Back To Black, It's The Original

Back To Black, It's The Beginning

Back To Black, It's Universal

Back To Black, It's The Cream

Back To Black, It's The Best

Back To Black, Soon You Will See

Back To Black, The Future Is Me

Back To Black, It's The Core

Back To Black, Say It Once More

Back To Black!!!!!

****

The Black Woman's Guide To Understanding Herself

Fear,

Insecurity,

And Pain

A Religion Of Fear

A Life Of Insecurity,

And A Love Of Pain

I, The Black Woman,

Am The Booty Of A Non-Hue Man,

A White Man

He Has Completely Captured

My Mind, Heart And Soul

I Am No Longer The Woman

Of A Hue-Man,

The Black Man,

Because My White Captor

Has Made My Entire Being Cold

It Is This Captor

Who Provides My Children And I

With The Necessities Of Life

And In Turn, Black Man,

We Disrespect You,

All The Days Of Your Short Life

Whatever My Captor Wants

His Morals, His Ways,

His Styles, His Religion

I Live!!!

Whatever He Says About

My Natural Man,

Whatever Filth He Hands Me,

I Give!!!

Though Unwillingly

I, The Black Woman, The Booty, The Ass,

The Prize For This Conqueror

Of The Black Man's Creation,

Am Frightened, Yet Strong,

And Crying Out To Regain Our Nation

In Reality, We Hate The Power

Of This Leprous, Pea-Brain, Primitive, Spineless, Low-Life, Devil,

Kind-Of-A-Man

(Not Man)

But He Is Skillful In Using His Tricks

On His Prize, Your Woman,

Your Creation, Your Universe,

To Keep You From Regaining The Power

Back Into Your Hand

With His Tricks,

He Has Programmed Your Woman,

His Booty,

To Use Her Tongue

To Keep You Maimed And Insane

Every Hour You've Been In This Land

And We Are Angry With You,

Black Man,

For Allowing This Half-A-Man To Capture Us

And Treat Us Like A Bitch!!

And All Our Anger Is A Plea To You

To Break This White Spell

That Makes Us Like A Wicked Witch!!

You Know, Black Man,

Even The Captor Is Tired Of The Wreck

That He Has Made Of Your Domain

And He Is Really Pleading With You
To Recapture What Is Rightfully Yours
Before He Goes
Uncontrollably Insane
Oh, Black Man, Kill This White Man
In Our Mind,
And Stop These Other Kind
Of Women From Capturing You
We Understand That All You Want
Is Peace Of Mind
But It Is Our Mind,
The Mind Of A Black Woman
That Can Bring You Real Peace
Only A Black Woman Can Nurture You
Into Becoming The King
Of The Civilizations,
And Even The King Of The Beasts
We Love You Black Man
Those Of Us
Who Really Want To Learn How To
And The More We Learn, We Realize That

The Entire Universe Needs You
To Take Control Of Her Again,
Better Than Before
Your Brotherhood And Unity
Will Recapture Us All,
And Bring Us Into Submission
To Your Righteous Will
Forever More
That Is Why
We Now Wish To Be Your Prize
To Admire You,
Boast About Your Greatness,
Your Tender Love,
Your Soothing Affection,
Charm, Command, And Protection
We Need You To Provide Us With
The Necessities Of Life,
Love And Direction
For The Benefit Of Yourself,
And Our God
The Black God,

The Lord Of All The Worlds

The One God,

The All In All

That Is All In You And Me,

Us,

We

I Hope You Now See

Just Say Be,

And It Is

I Want A Religion Of Peace,

A Life Of Unlimited Progress,

And A Love Of Respect And Honor

From A Man,

Amen,

A Black Man

I Want To Be Yours.

****

The Time

Wake Up, Black Man

It's Time For You To Rule

Wake Up, Black Man

Build Your Children Schools

The Devil Is Dying

He's Falling Very Fast

Can't You See That What He Has Will Never Really Last

Wake Up, Black Man

We're The Chosen One

Don't You Understand

That You Have Not Been Educated, But Trained

And Made To Be Like A Degenerate Hog

We're In This As One, Black Man

We've Been Bitten By The Same Dog

Your Woman Had Bared The Load

For 400 Years

Now We Destroy Our Babies

Because There's So Much Fear

How Can We Be Strong

When We're Delicate As Flowers

You're The One Who's Strong

You're The One With Power

Unite, Black Man

You Can Accomplish What You Will

Stray From The White Man

He Has Led You To The Kill

Wake Up, Black Man

Let's Unite As Sisters And Brothers

Wake Up, Black Man

We Need You

We Need Each Other.

****

Ah!! Peace At Last

I've Found What I've Been Looking For

In Righteousness And Peace

I Know You, And I Know Me,

And I Know Ungood Must Cease

In The Nation Of Islam

Where There Is Peace, Justice And Equality

The Positive Brothers And Sisters

Are Humble And Without Envy

We Have Heaven Here On Earth

And The Ultimate Is Hereafter

We Help Each Other

And All Our Mothers

But We Do For Self, First

With Happy Laughter

We Don't Need Pills Or Smoke

To Interfere With Our Minds

We Have Allah, Unity, And Love

And That's A Holy Find

So Come With Us Where All Is Peace

And Hypocrites Are Few To None
We've Come This Far
By Our Faith In All
And That's Why We're The One
I Say, "Oh Yeah," We're The One.
****

A Glimpse of Heaven

A Glimpse Of Heaven Is What I See
A Band Of Angels Walking With Me
Spirits Moved By Thoughts Of Peace
Joy And Happiness Shall Not Cease
Paradise Racing In Our Consciousness
Boundless, Vast, Infinite Progress
We're All Blessed
Our Visions Of God Are The Same
Called By His Name
Nay, Coming Down From Heaven
Yea, Up From Hell
With The Key To Lock Its Gate
We Excel
Above Poverty, Death, Distress
Negativity, Powerless
We Disbelieve In The Devil
So He Exists Not, On Any Level
Neither A Thought Nor Remembered
We're Compassionate And Even-Tempered

Peaceful And In Love With Life

Living 100s Of Years

With One Husband And One Wife

Earth, A Well-Balanced Heaven

The Look And Vitality Of 16

Even At Nine Hundred Seven

Never Altering In Age

Developed To The Highest Stage

A New World From Our Imaginations, Wondrous Creations

What We See, We Make Real

Our Thoughts Heal

The Doers Of Good On A Natural High

Regenerate Earth And Sky, And We Fly

Above The Clouds And Into Space

Sharing Wisdom Of The Human Race

With Other Beings Throughout Galaxies

If You See What I See

Let's Make Heaven A Reality

****

Prayer

Prayer Is The Perfect Mother

On Her, I Do Lean

She Nurtures Me To Strength

And From Such I Shan't Wean

Prayer Is For Allah

Between My Heart And Myself

He Provides My Health

And He Provides My Wealth

For On Allah, Is My Mind

So I Make Him My Guide

I Ask Him For His Blueprint

Because From Him I Am Designed

Prayer Keeps Me Straight

Makes Me Patient, So I Can Wait

For What I've Prayed

Prayer Is What I Breathe

What I Need

It Gives Me Faith In The Unseen

Prayer Is My Life. My Tears, It Wipes

When I'm Tired Out

It's My Second Wind

When I Feel In Doubt

It's My Loyal Friend

And Reminds Me Again

Prayer Is My Meditation

My Consultation

My Constant Meeting With My Lord

My Faithful Companion

No Longer Bored

I Bow, I Prostrate

And With A Low Voice I Utter

The Prescribed Words

At The Prescribed Times

Then I Open My Eyes

I See The Answers To My Right

And To My Left. Inside My Father

And My Sisters And My Brothers

Yes, Prayer Is The Perfect Mother

****

We Are One

We Come From Different Places

But Now We Are Together

In One Location

For One Purpose

We Are One

Like A Bouquet With Chrysanthemums

And Daisies, Violets, Roses, Gardenias,

Petunias, Sunflowers, Carnations

Together -- All Beautiful

We Come As Many

But Leave Synthesized

Like A Solid Brick Wall

We Are One

The Black And The Brown

And The Red And The Yellow

And The White And The Rainbow

Different Functions

But All Are Ready To Play The Same Tune

And Come Into Harmony

With His Song

We Are One

Not Here Just To Survive

But Here To Live

And To Enjoy The Abundance

And Riches Of Life

To Be Alive

We Are One

To Help Each Other Discover

Our Gifts And Talents

So That We All

Can Do

What We Are Borne To Do

And Come Into The Rhythm Of Life

We Are One

On One Planet

To Serve One God

Who Is Making Us Perfect

And Ready For A World Of

Unlimited Progress

Where There's One Mind

And One Family

And One Race

The Human Race

We Are One

****

One Verse, One Stanza, One Poem - Uni-Verse

I Am A Part Of One

The Moons, The Stars, The Planets, The Sun

Are All Stanzas In The Verse

Our Functions Are Diverse

But Our Tune Must Be

In Harmony

Doing The Will Of God

Is The Song We Must Play

Because It Is The Only Way

That A Uni-Verse Can Stay

****

Next Time, Produce A God

It's Time To Create Gods

From Our Wombs

Man Is Through

Produce Children

Who Will Rule

Create A Child

Who Will Make A Difference

Clean Up Your Seed, Your Egg

So That He Can Place His Mind

In Our Babies' Heads

Humanity Has Fallen

To The Level Of Savagery

Worshiping Things

The Creation

Not The Creator Do We See

Make A Nation

Who Will Teach

A Higher Way Of Civilization

No Need To Follow The Practices

Of Immoral Cultures And Traditions
For The Children Of God
Are To Lead The Whole Of Humanity
Into An Upward-Moving Condition
A Religion Is A Way Of Life
So Live On The Level Of God
Creating, Building
Replenishing, Growing
Not Like An Aimless River
Just Flowing
You Can Produce A God
With The Unlimited Capacity
To Beat All The Odds
Not Mass Murderers Or Serial Killers
Only Saviours And Healers
To Produce A God
Keep Good Thoughts In Your Mind
And Then The Earth We Live On
Will Be Just Fine

****

Soon

Envision There's No Sadness

It's Easy If You Smile

And No End To Kindness

It Will Be In A While

Envision Just Us, Right Here Living For This Moment

Envision No Perversions

And Nothing To Stop Our Reproduction

Nothing To Steal Or Lie For

And No Need For Us To Think Of Revolution

Envision Just Us, Right Here Living So Content

You May Say I'm A Dreamer

But So Are You, And You, And You

Maybe Someday You Will See It

And We Will Be As One

Envision No Cold Or Pollution

Just Clear Warmth Day And Night

And No Chemicals In Our Food

And No Need For Things That Are Not Right

Envision All Of Us, Right Here

Having Everything We Need

You May Say I Don't Know What I'm Saying

But You Say It All The Time

Maybe Someday You Will See It

And Then, We Will All Join Our Minds

****

The Kingdom Of Heaven Is Within You

Where Do You Think Heaven Is?

What Are You Looking For?

Do You Picture It In The Clouds?

Or Through A Golden Door?

The Kingdom Of Heaven

Is Like Unto A Thought

That Has Never Been Fulfilled

Thoughts Of Good, Peace, Beauty

Manifestations Of God's Will

The Kingdom Of Heaven

Is Like Unto Feelings

That Have Never Been Felt Before

New Feelings Of Kindness

Feelings That Would Take

A Strong Heart To Endure

The Kingdom Of God

Is Like Unto A New Civilization

After This World Loses It's Power

We'll Be Ready To Build

A Superior Nation
Building The Kingdom Of Heaven
Is Like Unto The Rising
And The Setting Of The Sun
Since The Beginning
We Are Sure That It Will Come
The Kingdom Of God
Is Like Unto A New Body
Your Body In It's Present Form
But You'll Be Taught
How To Preserve It
What To Put In It
And This Is Like Being Reborn
The Kingdom Of Heaven
Will Be On This Earth
For She Has Done Nothing Wrong
But Those Who Abuse Her
And Refuse To Do God's Will
Will Soon Be Long Gone
The Process Of Building
The Kingdom Of Heaven

Has Already Begun

So Accept Allah's New Way Of Acting

And New Way Of Thinking

And The Kingdom That Is Within You

Will Make Us All One

****

The Sun, The Son - The Light Of The World

His Spiritual Son

Is The Light Of The World

So Is His Physical Sun

Should You Serve The Light?

Or The Power Behind The Light?

The Son? Or The Father?

Do You Know His Name?

Do You Know What's Right?

The Son Asked,

"Why Callest Thou Me Good?

There's None Good But The Father..."

The Son Worshipped The Father,

And The Father Gave Him Power

These Are The Last Days

And This Is The Hour

That He Has Made Himself Known

You've Prayed For The Son

But The Father Has Come

And He Wants All Of Humanity

To Worship One

Him, Alone

What Is His Name?

Just Use Your Brain

The Son Spoke Arabic

Thus His Name Is Allah

And That Is Who The Son Called Upon

When He Had No One

He Didn't Worship Himself

He Worshipped The Father

And When You Serve The Father

You And He Become One

So Worship None But The One

Who Gives Power To The Son

We're His Children

And We Will Grow To Become

Just Like The Father Just Like The Son

We're His Reflection

Believe What You See

Look In The Mirror

You Will See Him In You

You Will See Him In Me

Worship The Son?

Worship The Power

That Gives Light To The Son

You Pray For The Return

Of The Son

He, Allah Is Present

And Since The Son And He Are One

The Son Has Come

Follow The Son And Just Like Him

You And The Father

Will Become One

****

All Women, Come Alive

We're Alive

We're Resurrected From The Dead

And We're Ready

To Accept His Head

We Heard The Trumpet

The Final Call

And Now We've Risen

From Our Great Fall

All Of His People, We Will Save

Lift Humanity From A Shallow Grave

And Change This World

Because We're Dissatisfied

That Our Girls Are Not Dignified

Men And Boys, Become Galvanized

Let's Quell The Weakness

Inside Of Us. Yes, It Must

Be Suppressed And Do Our Best

To Rule Without Guile or Vanity

And Humbly, Accept His Sanity

Use Aaron's Rod

To Return This Planet

Back To God

Because We're Alive And Ready To Strive

Against Those Who Disbelieve

In Their Own Power And Prefer To Cower

The Women Of God

Are On The Scene

We're Really Nice

But When We Have To

We Will Be Mean

We'll Never Again

Allow A Deceitful Snake

Steal Our Virtue

Yeah, We Will Hurt You

Because Hell Has No Fury

Like God's Woman's Scorn

This Is The Right Day To Be Born

Because We're Alive

We're Resurrected From The Dead

And If We Have To

We'll Take Some Heads

Oh, God, Allah, We Understand

Why You're Our First Man

Just Like Mary, You Will Use Us

To Bring Jesus … Back To The World

To Crush The Wicked

So We Can Live On This Planet

The Way You Planned It

Because We're Alive

We're Resurrected From The Dead

And We're Ready … To Accept Your Head

All Women Of God Come Alive

And Let's Rise … Let's Rise

****

I Am A Winner

Born To Win

Out Of The Millions

That Were Released

I Am The One

Who Swam The Fastest

And The Strongest

I Am The One

Who Met The Ovum Sitting There

Waiting To Die

Out Of The Millions

I Gave Her Life

I Am The One

Who Started The Metamorphosis

Inside The Darkness

I Am The Winner!!!

I Survived The Struggle

In A Hostile Environment

To Reach The Beginning

Of My Destiny

And Once I Made It

I Rotated And Evolved

And Emerged Into The Light

Inhaling The Breath Of Life

I Am The Winner!!!

Who Made It Through The Birth Canal

Into The World

To Proclaim To The World

That I Am Here!!!

There Is None Like Me!!!

The Original, The Winner, Born To Win!!!

I Am The Winner

And I Shall Win Again, And Again!!!

****

Awaken The God

We Are All Righteous Gods

Children Of The Most High

But We Had A Big Fall

We Took A Big Dive

But It's Been Heard

And It's Been Said

That Allah Is On The Scene

And It's Time

To Follow A Righteous Head

So Awaken The God In Your Heart

Awaken The God

In Your Soul

Awaken The God

In Your Mind

Awaken The God

And Join Onto Your Own Kind

The God In Us Has Slept

For Over 50 Thousand Years

Now We're Sitting On These Corners

Smoking Dope And Drinking Beer
What Happened Is
We Were Hit In The Head
By A Fiend
With Tricks And His Lies
We're Now Demented and Demeaned
We've Allowed The Jinn To Rule
For 6,000 Years
It Whispers Into Our Hearts
And Makes Us All Fear
But Now The Time Has Come
For Us To Rise
To Seek Refuge In God
And Bind The Serpent's Demise
So Awaken The God In Your Heart
Awaken The God
In Your Soul
Awaken The God
In Your Mind
When You Awaken The God
Peace And Self-Love You Will Find

One Reason Deceptive Intelligence

Is Still In Power

Is 'Cause People Are Asleep

Unaware Of The Hour

But Our Saviour Has Arrived

To Tell Us What Time It Is

It's Time To Awaken The God

So We'd Better Make It Our Biz

To Awaken The God In Our Hearts

Awaken The God

In Our Souls

Awaken The God

In Our Minds

When We Awaken The God

Only Admiration Will We Find

In Order To Awaken The God

You've Got To Pray And Think Good

Study Supreme Wisdom

'Cause It's All Good

The Nation Of Islam Is The Best Place

To Understand His Wisdom

And What He Requires Today

Most Of These Lip-Professors

Are Perpetrating A Fraud

They've Got You Worshiping The Son

And Not The Father, Allah

Why Would You Serve A Religion

That Condones Slavery

Islam Is Not For Cowards

It Will Make You Fearless and Free

So Give Beelzebub Back

His Names, Religions And Gods

Get Strong With Farrakhan, Elijah And Master Fard

And They'll Awaken The God In Your Heart

Awaken The God

In Your Soul

Awaken The God

In Your Mind

Awaken The God

And All That You Seek

You Shall Find

AWAKEN THE GOD!!!!

****

Made in the USA
Monee, IL
01 February 2023

25770585R00046